God's Truth
About
Climate Change

Don't worry, God's got this!

RENA BRITT

WestBow Press books may be ordered through booksellers or by contacting:

WestBow Press
A Division of Thomas Nelson & Zondervan
1663 Liberty Drive
Bloomington, IN 47403
www.westbowpress.com
844-714-3454

ISBN: 978-1-6642-8058-8 (sc)
ISBN: 978-1-6642-8056-4 (hc)
ISBN: 978-1-6642-8057-1 (e)

Library of Congress Control Number: 2022919024

Print information available on the last page.

WestBow Press rev. date: 01/30/2023

WESTBOW
PRESS®
A DIVISION OF THOMAS NELSON
& ZONDERVAN

God's Truth About Climate Change

Don't worry, God's got this!

Preface

Many of our children and adults are living with the fear that our earth will be destroyed by Climate Change. We frequently hear of the "existential threat" to our life. First, God does not want us to live in fear. Secondly, God tells us in His Word, the Bible, that this is not the truth. Not only will we not destroy our planet, we can't destroy it. God is preserving the earth until the day He chooses to end it and create a new heaven and a new earth.

With Covid, lockdowns, virtual learning, wearing masks all day at school, increased crime, isolation, depression and many other stressors, our children have more than enough issues with which to cope. As a counselor, I'm seeing a significant increase in the number of children and adults coming to receive psychological help.

It is important to help give security, coping skills and most importantly, God's truth to our children. That is a purpose of this book. "You shall know the truth and the truth will set you free." God wants us to be set free from the oppression of fear and scare tactics. God wants us to be good stewards and care for our beautiful earth, but not fall prey to the voices of the celebrities, politicians and scientists who claim life as we know it may end in seven years with the end of our planet.

God's plan for the earth:

The Beginning

> "In the beginning GOD created the heavens and earth." Genesis 1:1
> "Through Him, (Jesus) all things were made; without Him nothing was made that has been made." John 1:3

The Middle

> "Remember I am with you always." Matthew 28:20

> "For God so loved the world that He gave His one and only Son, that whoever believes in Him shall not perish but have eternal life." John 3:16

The End

> "The heavens will be set ablaze and the elements will melt with fire." 2 Peter 3:12

> "Then GOD will create a new heaven and a new earth for us." Revelation 21:1

1. **What does the world say about being afraid our earth will be destroyed by Climate Change? (When we say "World," we mean people on television, celebrities, athletes, politicians and most importantly, people who don't believe God and His Word, the Bible.)**

   1. The world says we need to live in fear that the earth won't exist much longer.
   2. They claim their opinions are proven facts.
   3. They assume we must believe them or else be blamed or silenced. Also, we may be labeled dumb and not scientific.
   4. They try to silence scientists who don't agree with them.

1. **What does Jesus say about being afraid the world will end because of Climate Change?**

   1. Don't be afraid, the Lord is with you.
   2. Be anxious for nothing.
   3. Do not worry about your life.
   4. Be strong and courageous.
   5. The highest heavens belong to the Lord, but the earth He has given to mankind.
   6. God tells us 365 times in the Bible to be not afraid.

We can trust Jesus to calm the storms

"...All men are created equal, that they are endowed by their creator with certain unalienable rights that among them are life, liberty and pursuit of happiness"

2. Why does the world want us to fear the earth will end from Climate Change?

1. If they scare us enough, we will listen to them, be discouraged and then do what they want us to do.

2. If we are really scared, we might start to agree with their solutions.

3. If we trust in them and their predictions, they can use tax money from us.

God's Word

2. What would Jesus say about believing their ideas about the earth ending?

1. Jesus wants us to trust Him first, not them.

2. Jesus does not want us to give up our God given freedoms and liberties to them or anyone.

3. Jesus does not want us to give up our money to people who don't know or speak God's truth. Only God can control the weather, the climate and the earth.

3. What does the world say about the earth being destroyed by flood?

1. The world believes the climate is warming so much that the ice caps will melt and our planet will be flooded.

2. The world believes it is our fault and we can control it.

God's Word

3. What would Jesus say about the earth being destroyed by flood?

1. God has promised He would never destroy the earth again by flood, as He did in the days of Noah, when Noah built the ark to survive.

2. God even gave us a symbol of His promise.

3. Do you know what that symbol is? It is the rainbow.

4. So, whenever you see a rainbow (or even a double rainbow) in the sky, you'll know you never ever have to fear the earth will be destroyed by flood.

5. God never breaks His promises.

Seed Time

Harvest Time

The Seasons

4. What does the world say about how the earth will end?

1. The world says the earth will be destroyed by flood.

2. The world says it will be destroyed by global warming or climate change.

3. The world says it will be destroyed by violent weather and natural disasters.

God's Word

4. What does Jesus say about how the earth will end?

1. God will never destroy the earth by flood. "And never again will I destroy all living creatures as I have done (by flood)." Genesis 8:21

2. God is preserving the earth until the day He ends it by fire and creates a new heaven and a new earth. "By the same word the heavens and earth that now exist are stored up for fire being kept for the day of judgement and destruction." 2 Peter 3:7 That means He will never let anyone else destroy it.

3. God says, "As long as the earth endures, seedtime and harvest, cold and heat, summer and winter, day and night WILL NEVER CEASE." Genesis 8:22 Seedtime and harvest tells us we will still be growing food. That lets us know we will have rain, not floods, sunlight, not extreme heat which would kill the plants. The climate and earth will remain the way He created it. Mankind won't be able to stop God's plan for His creation.

10

5. What does the world say about when the world will end?

1. They say it is imminent, it will end soon.

2. A former Vice President said, about three years ago, the world would be beyond repair in 12 years. That would mean we have about nine years left to save the planet.

3. A congresswoman said we have seven years left to save the planet.

4. The United Nations said in 1989 our world would end soon.

5. Throughout history, people of many sorts have predicted the end of the world, which we know of course has not come true.

5. What does Jesus say about the world ending?

1. No one knows when the world will end.

2. God will give us signs so we will know when the end is near. But those signs will be from Him, not from the world.

3. God already has a timetable and plan for the end of the world, as seen in the Book of Revelation, the last book in the Bible. So what the world says is meaningless and can't ever be true, if it goes against God's Word.

God's way

Man's way

6. What does the world say about taking care of the earth?

1. Respect it and keep it clean.

2. But do not use much of the bountiful and useful resources God has provided.

3. At times, the world puts the earth and animals above the needs of people.

4. At times, the world worships the creation and not the creator.

5. In many religions, people have worshipped the sun, moon, stars and manmade gods.

God's Word

6. What does Jesus say about taking care of the earth?

1. In ancient times, God had rules for how to care for the soil, by not planting crops in the seventh year. This would replenish the soil.

2. God wants us to appreciate the beauty of His creation and take care of it.

3. As God wants us to be responsible and kind to each other, He wants the same for His creation: a most wonderful and amazing gift to us.

7. What does the world say about who controls the weather?

1. The world says mankind can change and control the weather.

2. The world says when we have bad weather and earthquakes, very hot weather, very dry weather and storms, it can even be our fault.

3. Many people want to have power like God. It even started with Adam and Eve in the Garden of Eden.

God's Word

7. What does Jesus say about who controls the weather?

1. The Bible has 47 verses about Jesus being in charge of the weather. Jesus is "sovereign." That means He reigns or is in charge, not people.

2. Jesus got up and rebuked the wind and said to the sea, "Hush be still. And the wind died down and became perfectly calm." Mark 4:39-41

3. "He provides rain on the earth; He sends water on the countryside." Job 5:10

4. "He will give you rain for seed… your yield will be plentiful and your livestock will graze in a roomy pasture." Isaiah 30:23

5. God does not want people to try to have His power. He will always help us, but does not want us to think we can ever do what He alone can do.

Have children and fill the earth

God has blessed us with many natural resources for us to use in a clean way

God has also blessed us with natural resources for food

The world is in God's hands

16

8. What does the world say about who controls the planet?

1. The things we do can control our planet.

2. We have the power to destroy our planet.

3. If we use gas, oil, and coal (these are called fossil fuels), we can destroy the earth.

4. If we use these fuels to heat our homes, run our cars and our factories, we will be causing the death of our planet.

5. If we have too many people, it will hurt the earth.

8. What does Jesus say about who controls the earth?

1. Only God can control our planet.

2. People can't control the destruction of the earth, because God is saving it until the day He will end it by fire, not flood. He will create a new heaven and a new earth.

3. God has given us dominion over the earth. Dominion means we have a certain amount of power over the earth. God tells us to subdue the earth and use it to feed and take care of ourselves.

4. He has provided the fish of the sea, the cattle and animals, and the birds of the air for us to use.

5. He has provided us with land, water, seeds to grow vegetables and fruit and all these things in order to survive and enjoy.

6. God has provided us with the minerals, oils, gas and coal to take care of us.

7. "God blessed them and said to them, be fruitful and increase in number; fill the earth and subdue it..." Genesis 1:28 That means He wants us to have children and fill the earth.

8. God made the earth for us, not us for the earth.

9. God wants us to take good care of the earth.

9. What are some things you can say to others and yourself when you hear scary things about our earth being destroyed and coming to an end?

Some ideas and suggestions:

1. God tells me I don't have to be afraid. He says it 365 times.

2. God tells me He will never end the world by flood and I have the rainbow as His promise.

3. God tells me we will always have seasons, day and night, seedtime and harvest. That means we will always have food.

4. God always keeps His promises.

5. Only God can end the earth and create a new earth.

6. Some people in the world will lie to us to gain power over us.

7. Do I trust God's truth or what the World calls "truth?"

God will never let people destroy the earth because
He will create a new heaven and a new earth for us

God's Promise to Us

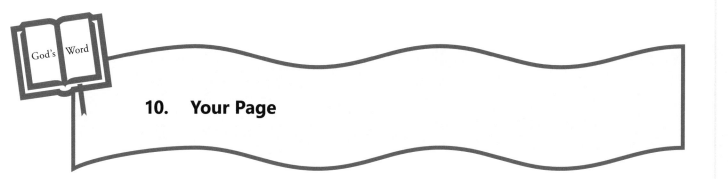

10. Your Page

Write some things you can say to feel safe about living in the world God created for us.

What are some pictures you can draw to show God's truth about Climate Change?

What are other verses in the Bible that tell about God controlling the weather?

Printed in the United States
by Baker & Taylor Publisher Services